GIANTS OF THE OLD TESTAMENT

LESSONS ON LIVING FROM
ISAIAH

A devotional by
WOODROW KROLL

BACK TO THE BIBLE®
Lincoln, Nebraska

CONTENTS

Day 1   The Trouble Within 4
Day 2   A Great Day Coming 6
Day 3   Tampering With the Contents 8
Day 4   In the Presence of Holiness 10
Day 5   Don't Be a Nobody 12
Day 6   The God of the Impossible 14
Day 7   A Light in the Darkness 16
Day 8   What's in a Name? 18
Day 9   The Rod of Jesse 20
Day 10   The Joy of My Salvation 22
Day 11   Trouble in the Evening 24
Day 12   Praise the Lord 26
Day 13   Perfect Peace 28
Day 14   Building on the Cornerstone 30
Day 15   The Quiet Spirit 32
Day 16   This Is the Way 34
Day 17   A Desert Rose 36
Day 18   The Eternal Word 38
Day 19   Those Who Wait 40
Day 20   Fear Not 42
Day 21   Compassion Fatigue 44
Day 22   The One and Only 46
Day 23   Held by His Hand 48
Day 24   In Old Age 50
Day 25   Never Forgotten 52
Day 26   Man of Sorrows 54
Day 27   Satisfaction Guaranteed 56
Day 28   Gotcha' God 58
Day 29   The Living Link 60
Day 30   Before You Call 62
Day 31   The God of Comfort 64

DAY 1

Isaiah 1:18

"Come now, and let us reason together," says the LORD, "Though your sins are like scarlet, they shall be as white as snow; though they are red like crimson, they shall be as wool."

The Trouble Within

A pastor discovered that the clock at the back of the sanctuary was unable to keep the correct time. Repeatedly he set the hands to the appropriate hour and minute only to find by the next week that it was either too fast or too slow. Finally he gave up and hung a sign above the clock that read, "Don't blame my hands. The trouble lies deeper."

That is where the trouble lies with us when we do wrong. We can blame our environment, our education, or even our parents, but the real trouble lies deep within our own hearts. Jesus said, "For out of the heart proceed evil thoughts, murders, adulteries, fornications, thefts, false witness, blasphemies" (Matt. 15:19).

Fortunately, God has provided a solution for that heart problem—the blood of Jesus Christ. Even the most crimson sin is washed away when the blood of Calvary's cross is applied. The apostle John wrote, "If we walk in the light as He is in the light, we have fellowship with one another, and the blood of

Jesus Christ His Son cleanses us from all sin" (1 John 1:7). And the writer of Hebrews says, "For if the blood of bulls and goats and the ashes of a heifer, sprinkling the unclean, sanctifies for the purifying of the flesh, how much more shall the blood of Christ, who through the eternal Spirit offered Himself without spot to God, cleanse your conscience from dead works to serve the living God?" (Heb. 9:13-14).

God assures you that no matter how colorful your sins may be, they can be washed white like snow. If you're still struggling with how to be cleansed from your sin and forgiven by God, accept what the Bible says as true. Confess your sins, ask for your heavenly Father's forgiveness and begin to live with a pure heart and a clear conscience. The difference is as striking as crimson and white.

Scarlet sins are no match for Christ's blood.

Reflections/Prayer Requests

_____

_____

_____

_____

DAY 2

Isaiah 2:4

He shall judge between the nations, and shall rebuke many people; they shall beat their swords into plowshares and their spears into pruning hooks; nations shall not lift up sword against nation, neither shall they learn war anymore.

A Great Day Coming

Peace has always been an elusive prospect. The *Columbia Dispatch* reported in 1993 that cable TV mogul Ted Turner funded a competition to find a book that gave a workable plan for world peace. Turner said he wanted to see if anybody had a real vision of a future world at peace and harmony. His quest ended in disappointment. He told an Atlanta gathering of news contributors to his Cable News Network's "World Report" that, "With 10,000 manuscripts, we did not have one plausible treatise on how we could get to a sustainable, peaceful future."

Apparently no one thought to check the Book of Isaiah. Here, God reveals that there is a day coming when wars will cease. This will not be the result of any plan proposed by the wisdom of man; it will come, instead, through the direct intervention of the Lord Jesus Christ. Revelation 20:1-3 foretells the imprisonment of Satan so that he "should deceive the nations no more till the thousand years were finished" (v. 3). During that time, the world will finally experience the peace it desperately needs. True peace can only come when the Prince of Peace brings it (Isa. 9:6).

We don't have to wait that long, however, to experience personal peace. That's available to you right now. When you trust Jesus Christ as Savior, you can have peace with God in your life immediately. The Bible says, "Therefore, having been justified by faith, we have peace with God through our Lord Jesus Christ" (Rom. 5:1).

World peace is a wonderful goal and it will be a great day when it happens, but personal peace right now is even greater. Peace among all the nations of the world will last only while Satan is imprisoned (Rev. 20:7-8). Our peace with God, on the other hand, will last forever (Ps. 16:11; 1 Thess. 4:17).

There has to be peace in the heart before there can be peace in the world.

Reflections/Prayer Requests

_____

_____

_____

_____

DAY 3

Isaiah 5:20

*Woe to those who call evil good, and good evil;
who put darkness for light, and light for darkness;
who put bitter for sweet, and sweet for bitter!*

Tampering With the Contents

On February 8, 1986, a Peekskill, New York, woman took a Tylenol capsule she had purchased at the local supermarket. Unknown to her, the bottle had been tampered with and the contents were contaminated with a lethal dose of potassium cyanide. Instead of helping her as she expected, the medicine took her life. Johnson and Johnson, the manufacturers of Tylenol, responded by removing the product from store shelves and reissuing the drug in caplet form contained in tamper-resistant bottles. These actions, however, could not alleviate the pain and grief of this woman's loved ones.

Millions of people have turned to the Bible to find relief from the pain of sin. Some, unfortunately, have not found the relief they sought. Instead they discover that people and churches have tampered with the words of Scripture, changing and adding to their meaning—even making what God says is evil appear to be good. For example, homosexuality is not a sin (Rom. 1:24-27), they claim, but an alternate lifestyle. Abortion is not murder (Ex. 21:22-25); it's a choice. What the Bible calls adultery, these people refer to euphemistically as "having an affair." Fornication is passed over as "living together." What is called drunkenness in God's Word is called the "disease of alcoholism" by a society bent on calling evil good and good evil. Obedience, on the other hand, is labeled as legalism, and zeal for the Lord is rejected as fanaticism.

Don't be fooled by this truth twisting. What God calls evil will never be made acceptable simply by using another word. Make sure that your beliefs are based on the solid foundation of God's Word. To keep your faith "tamper-proof," compare everything you hear with the Bible and see what God has to say. The Gospel is life-giving, but these additives and contradictions can be fatal.

Truth can't be improved with additives.

Reflections/Prayer Requests

_____

_____

_____

_____

_____

_____

DAY 4

Isaiah 6:2-3

Above [the throne] stood seraphim; each one had six wings: with two he covered his face, with two he covered his feet, and with two he flew. And one cried to another and said: "Holy, holy, holy is the LORD of hosts; the whole earth is full of His glory!"

In the Presence of Holiness

Dr. Bob Cook, president of the former King's College, New York, once mentioned that he had been at a gathering in Washington. While there he spoke with then-Vice President George Bush. Two hours later he chatted briefly with President Ronald Reagan. Smiling broadly, Dr. Cook added, "But that's nothing! Today I talked to God!"

Every Christian has the privilege of entering into the presence of God and speaking to the Sovereign Ruler of the universe. When we bow in prayer, the portals of heaven open and we have access to Him who sits on heaven's throne.

Isaiah's vision gives us some idea of what God's throne room must be like. It is a place permeated with the holiness of God. The seraphim standing above the throne cry out, "Holy, holy, holy." This thrice-repeated exclamation serves to emphasize the depths to which God's holiness exists. When we come before our Creator, we enter the intimate presence of a Holy God.

Is that how you approach God in prayer? Do you do so with the same sense of awe these seraphim have? They cover their face because God is too awesome and splendid to look upon. Even the highest of the angelic orders cover their feet before God in a gesture of humility. We must come into His presence with that same reverence. But like the seraphim, wings ready to fly at His command, you and I should also be prepared to proclaim His glory throughout the world. We come before Him with a sense of reverence, awe and obedience to serve. When we bow with these attitudes, we rise as more than conquerors (Rom. 8:37).

Holy praying requires a wholly pre-pared pray-er.

Reflections/Prayer Requests

DAY 5

Isaiah 6:8

Also I heard the voice of the Lord, saying:
"Whom shall I send, and who will go for Us?"
Then I said, "Here am I! Send me."

Don't Be a Nobody

Once upon a time there were four men named Everybody, Somebody, Anybody and Nobody. There was an important job to be done and Everybody was asked to do it. But Everybody was sure that Somebody would do it. Anybody could have done it. But Nobody did it. Somebody got angry about it, because it was Everybody's job. Everybody thought that Anybody could do it, and Nobody realized that Everybody wouldn't do it. It ended up that Everybody blamed Somebody and Nobody did the job that Anybody could have done in the first place.

Nobody is still alive and well in our churches. When the pastor pleads for someone to teach Sunday school, Nobody is the most likely one to respond. When clean-up day rolls around, Nobody reports for duty. When there is a need to provide housing for a visiting college chorale, Nobody is first in line. How refreshing it must be for God to hear Somebody say, "Here am I! Send me."

When Isaiah envisioned the Holy God and the spiritual need of the unholy world, he was energized to respond to the Lord's calling (Isa. 6:1-8). When he was released from the burden of his sin, he found a new enthusiasm for serving God. And so will you.

When you hear the summons to duty, don't avoid the opportunity—or Nobody will end up doing it. Instead of a Nobody, be the Somebody who is willing to respond enthusiastically to the opportunities of service to God. Instead of making excuses and letting others do the work, find the joy of being God's instrument to accomplish His will in the world.

Be God's Somebody; don't let Nobody get all the credit.

Reflections/Prayer Requests

DAY 6

Isaiah 7:14

*Therefore the Lord Himself will give you a sign:
Behold, the virgin shall conceive and bear a Son,
and shall call His name Immanuel.*

The God of the Impossible

Maybe you have seen the sign that says,
"The difficult is done immediately; the impossible takes a little longer." Those who display
such an advertisement are only engaging in
wishful thinking. But for God, doing the
impossible is a reality.

As Isaiah surrendered himself to be a mes-
senger for God (Isa. 6:1-8), he was given an
amazing prophecy. As a sign for his own day,
it was given as an encouragement for Ahaz,
king of Judah. Faced with threats from the
king of Syria and the king of Israel (2 Kings
16:5), Ahaz was fearful. But through the
Isaiah, God reassured him, saying, "Don't be
afraid. A child will be born and before this
child is old enough to tell right from wrong,
these enemies will be destroyed." And they
were. That child was born in 734 B.C. and
was about two years old when Rezin, king of
Syria, was killed by the Assyrians (2 Kings
16:9) and Pekah, king of Israel, was assassi-
nated by Hoshea (2 Kings 15:30).

Yet an even more amazing fulfillment lay
ahead. The prophecy had a near and far ful-

fillment. As Isaiah looked down the annals of history, he foresaw a day when God would do something that was truly amazing. Out of the womb of a virgin would come a child fathered by the Holy Spirit. Furthermore, He would be called Immanuel, which means "God with us" because He would be God, the second Person of the Trinity, and He would dwell with men and women. In a way that exceeds human understanding, God would compact Himself into the body of a baby and grow up to become a man. That man was Jesus Christ, God the Son, who would die for our sins.

In the same way, God can deal with the challenges of your life, whether they be merely difficult or totally impossible. He who brought forth His Son, born of a virgin, is more than adequate for anything that may be facing you.

Only God can take the "im" out of impossible.

Reflections/Prayer Requests

_____

_____

_____

_____

_____

DAY 7

Isaiah 9:2

*The people who walked in darkness have seen a
great light; those who dwelt in the land of the
shadow of death, upon them a light has shined.*

A Light in the Darkness

An artist created a painting of a wintry twi-
light. The trees were barren and laden with
snow while a dreary-looking house stood
desolate in the midst of the drifted field. It
was a bleak and depressing picture. Then the
artist took some yellow paint and with a few
quick strokes painted a candle glowing in one
of the windows of that home. The effect was
almost magical. Just one little light and the
entire scene was transformed into a vision of
comfort and cheer.

The prophet Isaiah looked at his own
country and recognized a need for comfort
and cheer. He saw the spiritual darkness that
enveloped many parts of his nation, especially in the north around the Sea of Galilee. This
area had been conquered by the Syrian king
Ben-Hadad (1 Kings 15:20) and became a
melting pot of Jews and Gentiles. A mixture of
Judaism and paganism became the dominant
religion. The situation looked hopeless, but
even into this stronghold of darkness and
spiritual death, Isaiah saw a light break forth.
Centuries later, when the apostles began to
preach the resurrected Christ, this area

became the center of a great revival (Acts 8:5-8). Indeed, the light of Christ's redemption shone brightly.

Whether it's your nation or your personal life, the light of Christ makes a difference. In the darkness of sin, you can find the light of His forgiveness. In the darkness of ignorance, His wisdom illumines the way. In the darkness of trials and trouble, His presence dispels the blackness. Whatever darkness threatens to overshadow your life, let Jesus be the light who drives it away. Jesus is the light of the world (John 9:5).

Wherever it is darkest, Christ shines the brightest.

Reflections/Prayer Requests

_____

_____

_____

_____

_____

_____

_____

_____

_____

DAY 8

Isaiah 9:6

For unto us a Child is born, unto us a Son is given; and the government will be upon His shoulder. And His name will be called Wonderful, Counselor, Mighty God, Everlasting Father, Prince of Peace.

What's in a Name?

Names are important. In fact, they are so important that the maker of Jelly Belly jelly beans puts the name of that candy on every little bean so consumers can distinguish them from "impostors." The chairman of the company said, "We want to guarantee consumers they are eating the best jelly beans on the market."

The same can be said for Jesus. There are many impostors who lay claim to the title of Christ. Billy Graham once noted that there are more than 2,000 people in the United States who claim to be a Messiah. Cult leaders such as Marshall Applewhite of Heaven's Gate and David Koresh of the Branch Davidians posed as Messianic figures, but led their followers to disaster.

Isaiah, however, says that the real Messiah will fulfill the roles of the Wonderful One, the Counselor, the Mighty God, the Everlasting Father and the Prince of Peace. Only one person has fulfilled all those names—Jesus

Christ. His counsel has been wonderful (Matt. 7:28-29; Mark 12:17). His power has been irresistible (Matt. 28:18). He has forever existed with the Father (John 1:1). And He alone is able to bring us peace (Rom. 5:1).

Don't be deceived by impostors. They may claim to be the Messiah, but they lack the obvious imprint of His names. They may appear to be genuine, but the apostle John warned, "Beloved, do not believe every spirit, but test the spirits, whether they are of God; because many false prophets have gone out into the world" (1 John 4:1). There is only one Messiah, the Lord Jesus.

Don't settle for less than the real thing—Jesus Christ.

Reflections/Prayer Requests

_____

_____

_____

_____

_____

_____

_____

_____

DAY 9

Isaiah 11:1-2

There shall come forth a Rod from the stem of Jesse, and a Branch shall grow out of his roots.

The Rod of Jesse

During World War II, Hitler's bombers rained destruction upon London from the skies. Over 15,000 people lost their lives and many parts of the city were reduced to rubble. Yet when spring came, an amazing thing happened. Beautiful wildflowers, many of them thought extinct, sprang up in the midst of the devastation. Botanists concluded that the seeds had laid dormant under buildings and other structures until the bomb blasts exposed them and gave them the opportunity to germinate.

Isaiah foresaw a day when Israel also would be devastated. The word for *stem* means a stump. David's lineage would be decimated. His mighty family tree would be chopped down to a stub.

Yet God would be faithful. Out of that "stump" would come the One who would be the Savior of the world. At a time when civilization lay devastated by the effects of sin, when the rubble of broken lives would be scattered over the countryside, a Branch from a tree long thought dead would appear with the promise of new life.

And so it happened. Paul declared, "But when the fullness of the time had come, God sent forth His Son, born of a woman, born under the law, to redeem those who were under the law, that we might receive the adoption as sons" (Gal. 4:4-5).

If the landscape of your life has been ravaged by discouragement and despair, look to Jesus, who is able to bring the hope of new life. Perhaps you have lost a loved one and life looks bleak. Maybe health problems have left you feeling like you're living in a war zone. Or family problems have created craters deep enough to swallow you whole. God will still be faithful to you. Give Him the "stump" of your life and watch Him grow a healthy and prosperous branch. Only the Rod of Jesse can give you such hope.

God can bring riches out of rubble.

Reflections/Prayer Requests

_____

_____

_____

_____

_____

_____

DAY 10

Isaiah 12:2-3

Behold, God is my salvation, I will trust and not be afraid; for YAH, the LORD, is my strength and song; He also has become my salvation. Therefore with joy you will draw water from the wells of salvation."

The Joy of My Salvation

Someone once asked Haydn, the famous church musician, why his music was so cheerful. He replied, "I cannot make it otherwise. When I think upon God, my heart is so full of joy that the notes dance and leap from my pen!"

Isaiah felt the same way. As he thought about the Lord, he reveled in the realization that God was totally trustworthy. He need never be afraid. No one could harm him when he was under the care of an omnipotent God. Furthermore, it was from this same God that he could draw his strength—not just physical strength, but the strength to face the trials and tribulations of life. Yet the crowning touch came as he considered that God was also the "well" of his salvation. Just as someone could draw life-saving water from a well in the ground, so Isaiah rejoiced that he could draw from the Lord the spiritual water he needed for his eternal life.

Such thoughts are the secret to a constant attitude of joy. But don't take your joy for granted. After David's sin with Bathsheba, God used the prophet Nathan to bring him to repentance. In the midst of his sorrow over his sin, David cried out, "Restore to me the joy of Your salvation" (Ps. 51:12). When David lost his fellowship with God, he did not lose his salvation, but he did lose his joy. And without the joy, our salvation is lacking an important ingredient.

Is your salvation a source of joy in your life? Do you delight in your relationship with God? If not, confess any sin that might be blocking that joy and then let your heart be filled with the joy that only God can give.

If there is no joy in your salvation, check what's in the well of your religion.

Reflections/Prayer Requests

_____

_____

_____

_____

_____

_____

_____

DAY 11

Isaiah 17:13-14

The nations will rush like the rushing of many waters; but God will rebuke them and they will flee far away, and be chased like the chaff of the mountains before the wind, like a rolling thing before the whirlwind. Then behold, at eventide, trouble! And before the morning, he is no more. This is the portion of those who plunder us, and the lot of those who rob us.

Trouble in the Evening

What do Assyria, Babylon and the Roman Empire have in common? All of them, at one time or another, conquered Israel. Yet they share another commonality—none of them exists today as a nation. You will never get an Assyrian stamp in your passport. No one will every proudly announce to you, "I'm a Babylonian!" None of these once-powerful nations has survived into the 20th century—but Israel has.

Throughout history men and nations have demonstrated their hatred for God's people. The Roman Emperor Diocletian is a good example. He issued an edict in 303 A.D. designed to annihilate the Christian religion and destroy the Bible. The emperor even built a monument on which were inscribed the words *Extincto nomene Christianorum* (The name Christian is extinguished). Only 25 years later, however, the emperor was dead, and the new ruler, Constantine, commissioned 50 copies of the Bible to be prepared at government expense.

Are you are facing persecution at work or school? Maybe people in your own family are seeking to discourage you from living out your Christian faith. God never promised that you wouldn't face these kinds of trials. What He did promise, however, was that ultimately those who afflict His people will fail. Your day of difficulties may seem long, but it won't last forever. Take heart! Morning is coming and when the sun rises, the night of despair is no more.

For every night of trouble, there's a morning of glory.

Reflections/Prayer Requests

_____

_____

_____

_____

_____

_____

_____

_____

DAY 12

Isaiah 25:1

*O LORD, You are my God. I will exalt You,
I will praise Your name, for You have done
wonderful things; Your counsels of old
are faithfulness and truth.*

Praise the Lord

William Law, in his *Serious Call to a Devout and Holy Life*, wrote, "Would you know who is the greatest saint in the world? It is not he who prays most or fasts most; it is not he who gives the most alms, or is best known for temperance, chastity, or justice; but it is he who is always thankful to God, who wills everything that God wills, who receives everything as an instance of God's goodness, and has a heart always ready to praise God for it."

Isaiah certainly fits Law's definition of a great saint. Even though this Old Testament prophet lived in a time of tremendous political upheaval, he never lost his sense of awe at God's greatness. He could see God at work doing "wonderful things." And despite the danger and peril that surrounded him, Isaiah was always ready to sing God's praises. He continually rejoiced in the knowledge that God's counsel is faithful and true.

Christians today live in a high-stress world as well. In some countries their physical lives are in danger. Kent Hill, executive director of The Institute on Religion and Democracy, said, "There have been more martyrs produced in the 20th century than in all the other centuries combined since the time of Christ." In the Western world the stress is more likely to come from rapid changes in technology and society. Yet these struggles produce anxieties and apprehension that are real as well.

What's the solution? Give yourself to praise. Whatever your situation, the all-powerful, all-knowing God of the universe is worthy to be exalted and glorified. Bill Bright, the founder of Campus Crusade for Christ, once said, "Something happens to the man who praises God; his life is blessed and enriched and he is strengthened." Let that be true of your life as well. Determine to take some quality time today just to praise the Lord. See if your day doesn't go better.

Faith runs best when oiled with praise.

Reflections/Prayer Requests

_____

_____

_____

_____

_____

DAY 13

Isaiah 26:3

You will keep him in perfect peace, whose mind is stayed on You, because he trusts in You.

Perfect Peace

Several years ago a submarine was being tested and had to remain submerged for many days. When it returned to port, someone asked the captain, "How did the terrible storm last night affect you?" The officer looked at him in surprise and exclaimed, "Storm? We didn't even know there was a storm!" The sub had been so far beneath the surface that it had reached the area known to sailors as "the cushion of the sea." Although violent storms might whip the ocean above into huge waves, the waters deep below are never stirred.

This is the promise that God gives to every believer who is willing to put his total trust in Him. The word for *perfect* that Isaiah uses means "complete, with no parts missing." God will give us a peace, not just in some circumstances but in all. We will have peace about our family, about our finances and about our health. When we surrender our lives to Him, the God of peace gives us a peace that "surpasses all understanding" (Phil. 4:7). It is a peace that guards both our hearts and our minds in Christ Jesus. It's a deep-down peace.

But this peace comes only to those who truly believe in and focus on the promises of God. The apostle James wrote that the person who allows doubts to cause division in his mind will be "like a wave of the sea driven and tossed by the wind . . . he is a double-minded man, unstable in all his ways" (James 1:6, 8).

As you read your Bible, be alert to the promises of God. Keep a list of those that are especially precious to you. Think about them. Meditate on them. Focus your attention on them. Pray back these promises to God, not as a reminder to Him, but as a reminder to yourself. If you fill your mind with His promises, God will fill your heart with His peace.

God's peace is for those who trust His purposes.

Reflections/Prayer Requests

_____

_____

_____

_____

_____

DAY 14

Isaiah 28:16

*Therefore thus says the Lord G*OD*: "Behold, I lay in Zion a stone for a foundation, a tried stone, a precious cornerstone, a sure foundation; whoever believes will not act hastily."*

Building on the Cornerstone

Historically, the cornerstone was the most important part of any building. The total weight of an edifice rested on this particular stone, which, if removed, would collapse the whole structure. The cornerstone was also the key to keeping the walls straight. The builders would take sightings along the edges of this part of the building. If the cornerstone was set properly, the stonemasons could be assured that all the other corners of the building would be at the appropriate angles as well. Thus, the cornerstone became a symbol for that which held life together.

In the days of Isaiah, the leaders of Israel had chosen to rest their security on a different cornerstone. They chose to put their trust in their own political savvy. Through various military alliances, they thought they could hold their nation together. Ultimately, however, this shaky cornerstone failed and Israel was taken captive by the Babylonians.

Yet God declared through Isaiah that He would establish a cornerstone that would never fail—a stone that could be trusted because it had been tried and proven to be precious and sure.

The New Testament writers recognized that this stone was Jesus Christ. The Savior said of Himself, "Did you never read in the Scriptures: 'The stone which the builders rejected has become the chief cornerstone'" (Matt. 21:42). The apostle Peter repeated Isaiah's prophecy and added, "And he who believes on Him will by no means be put to shame" (1 Pet. 2:6).

When the pressures of life bear down on you, there's only one cornerstone capable of handling the weight. When your need for guidance is urgent, there's only one cornerstone you can trust to keep your life straight. That cornerstone is Jesus. Trust Him with every aspect of your lives, and you will find that He never fails. He's not just a Rock; He's the Cornerstone.

A solid life begins with an immovable cornerstone.

Reflections/Prayer Requests

_____

_____

_____

_____

DAY 15

Isaiah 30:15

*For thus says the Lord G*OD*, the Holy One of Israel: "In returning and rest you shall be saved; in quietness and confidence shall be your strength." But you would not . . . .*

The Quiet Spirit

Human wisdom seldom produces the results that we desire. In an issue of *Meat & Poultry* magazine, the editors reported on a device used by the U.S. Federal Aviation Administration to test the strength of windshields on airplanes. The device launches a dead chicken at a plane's windshield at approximately the speed the planes flies. This indicates if the windshield could withstand a real collision with a bird during flight.

The British railway authorities were so impressed they borrowed the FAA's chicken launcher to test the windshield of one of their new high-speed train engines. In their test, however, the chicken not only went through the windshield but also the engineer's chair and embedded itself in the back wall of the engine cab. Stunned, the British asked the FAA to recheck everything to see if they had done anything wrong. After thoroughly checking it out, the FAA had one recommendation: "Next time, don't use a frozen chicken."

The people of Israel also were seeking solutions, but they, too, were looking to human wisdom. God noted that they trusted "in oppression and perversity" (v. 12). He called upon them to rest in Him, but they declared, "No, for we will flee on horses." Therefore God concluded, "those who pursue you shall be swift!" (v. 16). All their human wisdom would end in failure. When viewed objectively, human wisdom doesn't have much of a track record.

If you are going through a troubled time, stop trusting in human wisdom. Instead, let your spirit be quiet before God. Take the difficulties that are bothering you and prayerfully hand each one to Him. Leave them in His care and rest confident that He who loved you so much that He sacrificed His only Son for your salvation, also loves you enough to deal with whatever might be disturbing your heart today.

The key to a quiet spirit is a trusting heart.

Reflections/Prayer Requests

_____

_____

_____

_____

DAY 16

Isaiah 30:21

*Your ears shall hear a word behind you, saying,
"This is the way, walk in it," whenever you turn to
the right hand or whenever you turn to the left.*

This Is the Way

It used to be when you were lost that you stopped at a gas station and asked for directions. Hopefully the person who directed you knew what he was talking about. Technology, however, is changing all that. Rockwell International has produced the PathMaster system, which uses a satellite not only to beam route instructions to specially equipped automobiles but also allows the user to call up reviews of nearby restaurants and hotels. Etak Incorporated is offering a similar program, but in addition to travel directions it also keeps the driver up-to-date via satellite on possible traffic tie-ups and provides alternate routing instructions if necessary. The cost of these systems? Around $3,000.

Isaiah tells us, however, that there is a guidance system that takes no extra equipment or cash. All it takes is a heart sensitive to the still, small voice of God.

God has always been concerned with the direction in which mankind is headed. When He inquired of Adam in the Garden of Eden, "Where are you?" it was because He knew that Adam had veered off course. When the Israelites left the land of Egypt, He gave them a pillar of cloud by day and a pillar of fire by night so that they would not lose their way. Isaiah confessed that the people of his day were "like sheep [that] have gone astray; we have turned, every one, to his own way" (Isa. 53:6). But God did not give up on them. Instead He offered to restore them and give them the guidance they needed.

If you need God's guidance today, make sure your heart is right with Him. Then claim His promise. If you will listen to the voice of His Spirit, He will guide you through every twist and turn of your life's journey. He will tell you the way. Will you walk in it?

If you want to know God's way, you have to listen for His voice.

Reflections/Prayer Requests

_____

_____

_____

_____

_____

_____

_____

_____

DAY 17

Isaiah 35:1-2

The wilderness and the wasteland shall be glad for them, and the desert shall rejoice and blossom as the rose; it shall blossom abundantly and rejoice, even with joy and singing. The glory of Lebanon shall be given to it, the excellence of Carmel and Sharon. They shall see the glory of the LORD, the excellency of our God.

A Desert Rose

Boulder Dam was built in order to bring water to areas that had been desert. During the building of this dam, several workmen lost their lives. After its completion, a plaque was placed on the dam with the names of those who had been killed, with the following inscription: "These died that the desert might rejoice and blossom as the rose."

God revealed to Isaiah that Israel also would one day be restored. The land that had been devastated and destroyed until it was nothing more than a desert would be revived and become a place of beauty and fruitfulness.

To a certain degree, this prophecy has been realized. With the aid of technology and significant irrigation, Israel has restored many areas of the land to fruitfulness. Ultimately, however, Isaiah's prophecy will find fulfillment during the millennial reign of the Messiah. Then, not only will the nations beat their spears into pruning hooks (2:4) and the lion eat straw like the ox (11:7), but Israel will become an agricultural paradise. God promised it, so you can believe it.

Yet in a spiritual sense, this fulfillment can take place now. If your life has been a spiritual desert, Jesus can make it blossom. When you receive Him as your Savior, you become spiritually alive (Eph. 2:1). With the cultivation of the Holy Spirit, you will produce spiritual fruit a hundred times over (Matt. 13:23). Don't put that day off to some future time; do it now. Your life can blossom in the grace and mercy of God.

A surrendered heart is always a fruitful field.

Reflections/Prayer Requests

_____

_____

_____

_____

_____

_____

_____

_____

DAY 18

The Eternal Word

Very few things are permanent, no matter how solid they seem to be. Japanese scholar Chikaosa Tanimoto is now saying that the Sphinx, which has stood immovable on the Giza Plateau outside of Cairo, Egypt, for more than 4,500 years, is destined for destruction within the next 200 years. Because of erosion created by pollution and the forces of nature, the structure eventually will disintegrate into a heap of rubble. Other ancient monuments such as the great pyramids—Cheops, Chephren and Myceriuns—which were supposedly built to last forever, are also showing signs of crumbling. Given sufficient time, they also will return to the dust from which they came.

The same, however, cannot be said of God's Word. Even though portions such as the Book of Job and the five books of Moses (Genesis through Deuteronomy) are nearly 4,000 years old, they are as relevant today as the day they were written. Because the Bible deals with the nature of man and the love of God, it will always be applicable to man's need. Technology changes, cultures vary, fads come and go. But human nature stays the same, and the Bible always has the answer for man's deepest need.

Nor will Scripture ever lose its validity. The Bible is absolute truth, and truth doesn't change with time. Just as two plus two is four today, it was a thousand years ago and it will be a thousand years from now. The sins that offended the holiness of God when the Bible was written, such as adultery, homosexuality, lying and stealing, are just as sinful and offensive to a holy God today.

Other things may last a long time, even thousands of years, but only God's Word is forever. Every word of Scripture that you make a part of your life is an investment in eternity. Study it, memorize it, apply it—and your life will never be out of date.

Only the eternal Word can meet the needs of an eternal soul.

Reflections/Prayer Requests

_____

_____

_____

_____

_____

_____

DAY 19

Isaiah 40:31

Those who wait on the LORD shall renew their strength; they shall mount up with wings like eagles, they shall run and not be weary, they shall walk and not faint.

Those Who Wait

People in the United States hate to wait. Some define a split second as the time between the traffic light turning green and the person behind you blowing his horn. Fast-food chains have sprung up everywhere because many people don't want to go to restaurants where they have to wait for their food. Grocery stores have express lanes so that those with only a few items will not have to wait long. Patience is certainly a dying virtue in our culture.

God knew that Israel would have to wait a long time for fulfillment of the many promises He gave through the prophet Isaiah. Nearly 150 years would pass before "Cyrus . . . My shepherd" would restore the people from captivity (44:28). It would be more than 700 years before the "people who walked in darkness" would see the light of the Gospel (9:2). And many promises have yet to be fulfilled (11:6-9; 35:1-10).

We may not like to wait, but God attaches a promise to waiting. In patiently trusting

Him, He assures us, we will find a new strength. When the right time comes, we will have wings like eagles and supernatural endurance.

Many Christians wear themselves out because they are running ahead of God rather than waiting for His perfect time. If you're prone to do this, let God not only have His will in your life, but also let Him accomplish that will in His time. Use the waiting time as an opportunity to renew your strength and prepare for what lies ahead. Waiting doesn't have to be a drag; it can be a surge.

It's better to be renewed by waiting than ruined by rushing.

Reflections/Prayer Requests

_____

_____

_____

_____

_____

_____

_____

_____

_____

DAY 20

Isaiah 41:10

*Fear not, for I am with you; be not dismayed,
for I am your God. I will strengthen you,
yes, I will help you, I will uphold you
with My righteous right hand.*

Fear Not

As an old farmer sat on his front porch, a stranger came along and asked, "How's your cotton coming?" "Ain't got none," he replied. "Didn't plant none. 'Fraid of the boll weevil." "Well, how's your corn?" "Didn't plant none of that either. 'Fraid o' drought." "How about your potatoes?" "Ain't got none. Scairt o' tater bugs." The stranger finally asked, "Well, what did you plant?" "Nothin," answered the farmer. "I just played it safe."

Isaiah was not called to "play it safe." Instead, God called him to confront kings (7:3) and denounce mighty nations (34:1-2). All around him vast armies were on the move, and political scheming was rampant. Yet in the midst of all these intimidating situations, God said, "Don't be afraid. I am with you."

There are many things that cause fear; in fact, someone has estimated that the average person has at least 200 fears. Yet the answer to all of them is the same—God. As the hymn writer so aptly put it, "Fear not, I am with thee—O be not dismayed, for I am thy God, I will still give thee aid. I'll strengthen thee, help thee, and cause thee to stand, upheld by my gracious, omnipotent hand."

If God has called you to something, don't be afraid. If He has called you to be single, don't be afraid. He will stand in the gap. If He has called you to live alone, don't be afraid. His company will comfort you. If He has called you to serve Him far from family and friends, don't be afraid. He will be there for you. God has not called us to play it safe; He has called us to trust Him.

Where God has called us, He will keep us.

Reflections/Prayer Requests

_____

_____

_____

_____

_____

_____

_____

_____

_____

_____

DAY 21

Isaiah 42:3

A bruised reed He will not break, and smoking flax He will not quench; He will bring forth justice for truth.

Compassion Fatigue

An Irishman was down on his luck and was panhandling on Fifth Avenue before the annual St. Patrick's Day parade got underway in New York City. As a couple strolled by, he called out, "May the blessing of the Lord, which brings love and joy and wealth and a fine family, follow you all the days of your life." There was a pause as the couple passed his outstretched hand without contributing. Then he shouted after them, "And never catch up to you!"

Perhaps we can identify with that couple. Our mailboxes are stuffed with appeals from various organizations; our phones ring with individuals seeking pledges; some people even come right to our doors with solicitations. After a while, we can fall into an attitude that sociologists call "compassion fatigue." It simply means we turn our back even on worthy causes because we can't handle another request.

Fortunately, God never suffers from such an ailment. No matter how often we go to Him with our needs, He never turns us away.

His compassion is always available. He treats us as one who is as tender as a bruised reed or as fragile as smoking flax.

Christians need to take care that we do not become fatigued in our compassion. The apostle Paul exhorts us, "And let us not grow weary while doing good, for in due season we shall reap if we do not lose heart. Therefore, as we have opportunity, let us do good to all, especially to those who are of the household of faith" (Gal. 6:9-10).

With limited time and funds, we must prayerfully ask the Lord what He would have us do when we are presented with an opportunity to give. Once we know His will, however, let nothing keep us from showing compassion. Succumbing to compassion fatigue can squelch the work of God.

Duty makes us do things well; compassion makes us do them beautifully.

Reflections/Prayer Requests

_____

_____

_____

_____

_____

_____

DAY 22

Isaiah 44:6, 8

*Thus says the L*ORD*, the King of Israel, and his Redeemer, the L*ORD *of hosts: "I am the First and I am the Last; besides Me there is no God. . . . Is there a God besides Me? Indeed there is no other Rock; I know not one."*

The One and Only

Michel Lotito of Grenoble, France, is one of the most unusual individuals in the world, at least when it comes to his culinary tastes. Since 1959, at the age of nine, Mr. Lotito has daily dined on metal and glass. According to *The Guinness Book of Records*, he consumes two pounds of metal per day. So far he has eaten, among other things, ten bicycles, a supermarket cart, seven TV sets, six chandeliers, a low-calorie Cessna light aircraft and a computer. Few have cared to match his record.

Michel Lotito is unusual, but God is more than unusual; He is unique. There are no others like Him. The God of all knowledge declares, "Is there a God besides me? Indeed there is no other rock; I know not one." No one is able even to come close to matching His deeds.

Yet in spite of his uniqueness, this singular Person of the universe has declared His love for you and me. He offers Himself as our rock, a place of safety and stability. He is the rock of our salvation (Ps. 95:1), the rock of refuge (31:2), the rock of our strength (62:7) and the rock that is "higher than I" (61:2). He is the one and only Person able to meet all our needs.

If you do not know this one and only God, you can. He has revealed Himself in many ways, most especially in His Son, Jesus Christ. When you come to know Jesus as your Savior, you come to know God as the One and Only God. Why not surrender your life to Him today?

There are many pebbles, but only one Rock.

Reflections/Prayer Requests

DAY 23

Isaiah 45:1

Thus says the LORD to His anointed, to Cyrus, whose right hand I have held—to subdue nations before him and loose the armor of kings, to open before him the double doors, so that the gates will not be shut.

Held by His Hand

A pastor once shared that when his son was small, they often walked together through the fields and neighboring pasture behind the parsonage. At first the little fellow would hold onto his father's finger, but he found that when he stepped into a hoof print or stumbled over something, his grip would fail and he'd fall to the ground. This happened quite frequently until one day he looked up at his father and said, "Daddy, I think if you would hold my hand, I wouldn't fall." The pastor reflected, "You know, he was right. He still stumbled many times after that, but he never hit the ground."

Cyrus the Great, the one whom God would use to return His people from Babylon, had the same experience. As a leader he would face many challenges. It was first necessary that he weld two peoples, the Medes and the Persians, into a united kingdom. Accomplishing that, he then set out on a path of conquest that ultimately brought him to Babylon, the city thought to be impregnable. Ingeniously, the river Euphrates was diverted and Cyrus' army slipped into the city through the dried-up river bed and conquered it. Through it all, although Cyrus didn't know it, God held his hand.

The future is sure to contain trials and difficulties for you. Maybe you've already encountered some of them. If you try to hold on to God's hand, the likelihood is great that you will slip and stumble. The better solution is to let God hold your hand. Instead of striving and straining, let go and let God hold onto you. Surrender yourself to God and trust Him to keep you secure.

Let Him who holds everything else hold your hand as well.

Reflections/Prayer Requests

_____

_____

_____

_____

_____

_____

_____

_____

DAY 24

Isaiah 46:4

Even to your old age, I am He, and even to gray hairs I will carry you! I have made, and I will bear; even I will carry, and will deliver you.

In Old Age

The U.S. Census Bureau has declared the year 2020 as the beginning of the age of the elderly. The 65 and older segment of our population will increase from one in eight Americans today to one in six by that date and one in five by 2050. By the beginning of this new era, the nation's elderly will total 53.3 million—a 63 percent increase over the current elderly population of 33 million. It would appear that the United States is destined to become a nation of the aged.

Yet the very thought of old age strikes fear in the hearts of many people—perhaps with good reason. Old age brings with it health concerns as the body deteriorates, financial concerns with the onset of retirement and even social concerns as friends and relatives die. Just the thought of such dramatic changes is a terrifying prospect to some.

In the midst of all this, however, God promises that He will never change. Even though you experience many changes as you grow older, He will stay the same. The writer of Hebrews reminds us that "Jesus Christ is the same yesterday, today, and forever" (Heb. 13:8). Just as He saw you through the crises of youth and middle age, so He will see you through all the challenges of growing old. When your strength fails, just remember that He promises to carry you. When you feel trapped inside an aging body, remember that He who sustains you today will continue to bear you throughout all your days.

The God of the ages is also the God of the aged.

Reflections/Prayer Requests

_____

_____

_____

_____

_____

_____

_____

_____

_____

_____

DAY 25

Isaiah 49:15-16

*Can a woman forget her nursing child, and not
have compassion on the son of her womb?
Surely they may forget, yet I will not forget you.
See, I have inscribed you on the palms of My
hands; your walls are continually before Me.*

Never Forgotten

I can empathize with the man who said, "I
write down everything I want to remember.
That way, instead of spending a lot of time
trying to remember what it is I wrote down, I
spend the time looking for the paper I wrote
it on." Most of us are able to forget much better than we remember.

Yet God assures us that He will never forget us. Not for a second are we ever out of His
thoughts. In fact, Isaiah tells us that we are
inscribed on the very palms of His hands—the
part of our body we use to reach out and
demonstrate our love and concern through
the ministry of touch. And the palms are the
most tender part of those hands. So it is with
compassionate and tender love that God has
engraved us on His divine palms.

Sometimes in the midst of our troubles it
may seem as if God has overlooked us. We
pray and God doesn't seem to hear us. We
read our Bibles, but the verses all seem lifeless and meaningless. We look for solutions,
but God provides no answers.

Despite your circumstances, remember where your name is engraved. Be assured that God has not forgotten you. The forgetfulness that is so common with humans can never afflict Him. Jesus' nail-pierced palms are vivid reminders of our infinite value and His unending love. Give God time to accomplish His purpose in your life. Have confidence that your situation is only temporary. Stand firm on God's promise, "Yet will I not forget you." You're in good hands with God.

God always oversees; He never overlooks.

Reflections/Prayer Requests

_____

_____

_____

_____

_____

_____

_____

_____

_____

_____

_____

DAY 26

Isaiah 53:3-4

He is despised and rejected by men, a man of sorrows and acquainted with grief. And we hid, as it were, our faces from Him; He was despised, and we did not esteem Him. Surely He has borne our griefs and carried our sorrows; yet we esteemed Him stricken, smitten by God, and afflicted.

Man of Sorrows

Ted Turner, founder of Cable News Network, spoke in Orlando, Florida, a few years back and told a very moving story. Turner mentioned that he was raised in a God-fearing family and had a sister who was ill. Her illness progressed; she became critical. He prayed desperately for the Lord to spare her life and make her well. But she died. Then Turner told the audience that from that point on he knew, even as a kid, there was no God. What kind of loving God would have allowed his sister to suffer and die? Since that experience, he said, he has depended upon himself, not on an unfeeling, phantom-being that does not exist.

It's sad that Turner's perspective on God became skewed. Isaiah gives us a much different insight. The prophet does not say that God removes our sorrows; instead He sent someone to bear them with us—the Lord

Jesus. He is acquainted with our griefs because He experiences them along with us. For reasons beyond our comprehension, God chose to link His happiness to ours. When we hurt, He hurts.

What a great blessing this is! The writer of Hebrews says, "For we do not have a High Priest who cannot sympathize with our weaknesses, but was in all points tempted as we are, yet without sin. Let us therefore come boldly to the throne of grace, that we may obtain mercy and find grace to help in time of need" (Heb. 4:15-16).

How can you be sure you will find mercy and grace? Because God experiences your pain right along with you. He understands how you feel. So come boldly, not with the expectations that God will always remove your pain, but with the assurance that He will bear it with you.

The sorrow and grief that Christ bore were not His but yours.

Reflections/Prayer Requests

_____

_____

_____

_____

DAY 27

Isaiah 55:1-2

Ho! Everyone who thirsts, come to the waters; and you who have no money; come, buy and eat. Yes, come, buy wine and milk without money and without price. Why do you spend money for what is not bread, and your wages for what does not satisfy? Listen diligently to Me, and eat what is good and let your soul delight itself in abundance.

Satisfaction Guaranteed

An anonymous author who had lived for the fleeting things of this world penned the following lines: "How foolishly I have employed myself! In what delirium has my life been passed! How I've wasted my life while the sun in its race and the stars in their courses have lent their beams—perhaps only to light me to perdition! I have pursued shadows and entertained myself with dreams. I might have grazed with the beasts of the field, or sung with the birds of the woods, to much better purposes than any for which I have lived."

What a contrast to those things which God has to offer. Not only are the portions from His table free and abundant, but most important, in the end they satisfy. Instead of regret, they result in joy and satisfaction.

Jesus told the Samaritan woman at the well, "Whoever drinks of the water that I shall give him will never thirst. But the water that I shall give him will become in him a fountain of water springing up into everlasting life" (John 14:4).

Israel had to learn this truth the hard way. In spite of Isaiah's pleas, the people chose to chase after material well-being and political security rather than turn their hearts to the Lord. In the end, they lost everything as they were carried away to Babylon.

Are you looking for satisfaction? Then open your Bible and partake of the feast that God has spread for you. His promise is that when you reach the end of your life, you will never regret a moment that you have spent at His table.

With God, satisfaction is always guaranteed.

Reflections/Prayer Requests

_____

_____

_____

_____

_____

DAY 28

Isaiah 55:8-9

"For My thoughts are not your thoughts, nor are your ways My ways," says the LORD. "For as the heavens are higher than the earth, so are My ways higher than your ways, and My thoughts than your thoughts."

Gotcha' God!

A young boy at the dinner table asked, "Dad, is God everywhere?" "Yes," his father assured him, "God is everywhere." "Is He in this room?" the boy wanted to know. "Of course," his father said. "If God is everywhere, then He is in this room." Eyeing the sugar bowl on the table, the boy continued, "Well, is God in that sugar bowl?" "Yes," his father replied, "if God is everywhere, I guess we'd have to say that He's even in the sugar bowl." Reaching for the lid, the boy quickly slipped it over the bowl. "Gotcha', God!" he said.

The Israelites also wanted a "sugar bowl" god, someone they could control. Isaiah rebuked them for cutting down a tree and using part of it to warm themselves and with the rest making it "into a god, His carved image. He falls down before it and worships it, prays to it and says, 'Deliver me, for you are my god!'" (44:17). Israel wanted a god who could be contained in their temples and manipulated by their worship—but the God Isaiah had seen (6:1) was not that kind of a God.

How wonderful to know that the real God is so much greater than anything we can imagine or create. His ways and even His thoughts are so far beyond our finite minds that we can't begin to comprehend Him. When we come to Him with our problems and our difficulties, we never have to worry about whether He's big enough to handle them.

Don't try to put God in a sugar bowl. You won't be successful, for He is an awesome God. Rejoice that though you may not be able to understand Him, you will always be able to trust Him.

God will be God regardless of what we do!

Reflections/Prayer Requests

_____

_____

_____

_____

_____

_____

_____

_____

DAY 29

Isaiah 59:2

But your iniquities have separated you from your God; and your sins have hidden His face from you, so that He will not hear.

The Living Link

Great Britain's King George V was to give the opening address at a special disarmament conference with the speech relayed by radio to the United States. As the broadcast was about to begin, a cable broke in a New York Radio station and more than a million listeners were left without sound. A junior mechanic in the station, Harold Vivien, solved the problem by picking up both ends of the cable and allowing 250 volts of electricity to pass through him harmlessly. He became a living link.

Sin causes the same problem as a broken cable. It interferes with our ability to communicate with the King of the universe. In fact, Isaiah goes so far as to say that sin separates us from God.

Fortunately, a provision has been made to bridge that break. Just as Mr. Vivien became the means for communication to be restored with King George V, the Lord Jesus Christ has become the link to reconnect us to God. The apostle Paul wrote, "He [God] has delivered us from the power of darkness and translated us into the kingdom of the Son of His love, in whom we have redemption through His blood, the forgiveness of sins" (Col. 1:13-14).

When our sins are covered by the blood of Christ, God can communicate with us through His Word. Instead of being dull, lifeless words on a page, they are infused with spiritual vitality that can change our lives. Furthermore, our own communication with God—prayer—becomes unfettered. We have the assurance that He hears us and will respond to our needs.

If you feel like you aren't getting through to God, maybe the link is broken. Ask Him to show you any sin in your life that might be hindering your ability to communicate with Him. Then confess it, forsake it, and get back in communication with the King.

The Living Link is the only solution to the broken link.

Reflections/Prayer Requests

_____

_____

_____

_____

_____

DAY 30

Isaiah 65:24

It shall come to pass that before they call, I will answer; and while they are still speaking, I will hear.

Before You Call

Dr. Helen Roseveare, a missionary to Africa, told about a mother who died at the mission station after giving birth to a premature baby. An incubator was set up to keep the infant alive, but the only available hot water bottle was beyond repair. During devotions that morning the children were asked to pray for the baby and for her young sister, who were now orphans. One of the girls responded, "Dear God, please send a hot water bottle today. Tomorrow will be too late because by then the baby will be dead. And dear Lord, send a doll for the sister so she won't feel so lonely."

That afternoon a large parcel arrived from England. Eagerly the children watched as it was opened. Much to their delight, under some clothing was a hot water bottle! Immediately the girl who had prayed so earnestly started to delve deeper, exclaiming, "If God sent that, I'm sure He also sent a doll." And she was right! Five months earlier, God had led a group of women in England to include both of those items in response to a prayer that had not yet been uttered.

That's the promise God gives us through Isaiah. As the One who knows what lies ahead, the Lord works even in the past to bring about blessings for His children's future.

As you consider your situation today, it may seem that the Lord is asking you to do the illogical. You may think, *Why should God prompt me to do this? I see no need.* But remember, what you do today could be the answer to someone's prayers tomorrow. Trust God, and let the One who holds both the past and future be your Guide for the present.

With God, the past and future are simply part of the eternal present.

Reflections/Prayer Requests

_____

_____

_____

_____

_____

_____

_____

_____

_____

DAY 31

Isaiah 66:13

As one whom his mother comforts, so I will comfort you; and you shall be comforted in Jerusalem.

The God of Comfort

A mother said that her little girl, who was terrified of the dark, slept at night in a crib beside her bed. Often the mother had been wakened during the night by a little voice saying, "Momma, it's dark! It's dark, Momma! Take Sally's hand." And when, in answer to her cry, the mother took hold of her tiny hand, the little girl would sink quietly back to sleep, all her fears being removed.

The Israelites, too, were beset with fears: political uncertainty surrounded them, and even greater tragedies lay ahead. Isaiah foresaw the day when the nation would be overrun by the Babylonians, with many people killed and most of the rest taken into captivity (39:6-7). It would be a time when they would need the special comfort that mothers are so good at giving. And in the midst of the darkness of those days, God assured them that He would be there to comfort them.

If you are needing comfort, be assured that God is also there for you. The apostle Paul declared, "Blessed be the God and Father of our Lord Jesus Christ, the Father of mercies and *God of all comfort*, who comforts us in all our tribulation" (2 Cor. 1:3-4, emphasis mine).

Perhaps you are experiencing the deep night of bereavement. Maybe the inky blackness of physical infirmities has closed around you. Whatever might be the cause of your sorrow, don't hesitate to lift your heart to the Lord and say, "Father, it is dark! Take my hand." Reach out and let Him enfold your hand in His. You will find a comfort that no one else can bring. God's strong hand is only a prayer away.

You can experience all the comfort of God through the God of all comfort.

Reflections/Prayer Requests

_____

_____

_____

_____

_____

_____

_____

_____

_____

_____